EDGE BOOKS

DIRT BIKES

Travis Pastrana
Motocross
Legend

by Terri Sievert

Consultant:

Alex Edge
Associate Editor
MotorcycleDaily.com

Capstone
press

Mankato, Minnesota

Edge Books are published by Capstone Press,
151 Good Counsel Drive, P.O. Box 669, Mankato, Minnesota 56002.
www.capstonepress.com

Library of Congress Cataloging-in-Publication Data
Sievert, Terri.
    Travis Pastrana: motocross legend / by Terri Sievert.
    p. cm.—(Edge books. dirt bikes)
    Summary: "Traces the life and career of motocross racing and motocross freestyle star
Travis Pastrana"—Provided by publisher.
    Includes bibliographical references and index.
    ISBN 0-7368-4367-1 (hardcover)
    1. Pastrana, Travis, 1983-—Juvenile literature. 2. Motorcyclists—United States—
Biography—Juvenile literature. 3. Motocross—Juvenile literature. I. Title. II. Series.
GV1060.2.P39S54 2006
796.7'5'092—dc22   2005005812

Editorial Credits
Connie Colwell Miller, editor; Jason Knudson, set designer; Kate Opseth,
    book designer; Wanda Winch, photo researcher; Scott Thoms, photo editor

Photo Credits
Corbis/NewSport/Larry Kasperek, 9
Frank Hoppen, cover, 5, 6, 11, 14, 20, 27
Getty Images Inc./Jeff Gross, 23
Steve Bruhn, 13, 17, 18, 24, 28

1 2 3 4 5 6 10 09 08 07 06 05

Table of Contents

CHAPTER 1

A Grand Stunt

On November 14, 2001, Travis Pastrana sat on his motorcycle on the edge of the Grand Canyon. Rocky cliffs and steep drops surrounded him. He was about to make the most dangerous motorcycle jump of his life.

Learn about:

- Grand Canyon jump
- Gold medals
- Into the bay

Many people consider Travis the best freestyle rider in the world.

Travis' daring moves attract the attention of fans everywhere.

Travis took off. He rode straight over the edge of a 1,500-foot (457-meter) cliff. While in the air, Travis spun his motorcycle upside down to do a backflip. He swung his legs to one side of the bike and clicked his heels. He then let go of his bike. He opened a parachute and floated safely to the ground. Travis performed the trick he had been dreaming of since he was 10 years old.

Motocross Moves

Travis Pastrana is considered the best freestyle motocross rider in the world. He has won gold medals in the X Games and the Gravity Games.

"Jumping into the Grand Canyon was one of the greatest thrills of my life."
—Travis Pastrana

Travis is known for performing thrilling stunts during competitions. He often lets his legs fly out behind him during motorcycle jumps. He was one of the first motorcycle riders to do a backflip on his bike.

In 1999, Travis thrilled the crowd at the X Games competition. After winning the gold medal, he zipped over a dirt ramp and rode his motorcycle into San Francisco Bay. He had to spend some of his prize money to have the bike fished out of the water. But Travis didn't mind. He enjoyed entertaining the crowd.

Travis impresses crowds with his daring tricks.

CHAPTER 2

Following His Heroes

Travis was born October 8, 1983, in Annapolis, Maryland. When he was 4 years old, he received a Christmas present that changed his life. His parents gave him a Honda Z-50 motorcycle. Travis' father taught him to ride the small one-speed motorcycle.

Learn about:
- A Christmas gift
- Amateur champion
- A new star

Travis spends many hours practicing his moves.

First Events

Travis quickly became interested in motorcycle racing. He watched pro riders like Jeremy McGrath and attended their races. He waited around after the races to get autographs from his favorite riders.

Soon, Travis began competing in motocross races of his own. He was one of the first riders to perform daring tricks during motocross races.

Travis enjoyed doing the tricks. People enjoyed watching Travis perform freestyle moves like the no-footed backflip. To perform this move, Travis flipped his bike backward in the air while sticking his feet straight out. He also performed the Superman. In this move, Travis lifted his legs straight out behind him as the bike soared through the air.

Winning Events

Travis soon dominated freestyle motocross. He won five amateur national championships between 1992 and 1999. In 1998, at age 14, he became the World Freestyle Champion.

Travis enjoys performing tricks such as the Superman.

Travis' daring tricks made him a motocross superstar.

In 1999, Travis entered his first pro race. He competed in a race called the Rose Bowl World Supercross in Pasadena, California. He was only 16 years old when he took first place in this race. Travis was on his way to becoming a motocross superstar.

"My strengths and weaknesses are the same: I've got the willingness and stupidity to try anything. If I think it's even remotely possible, I'll do it."
—Travis Pastrana

CHAPTER 3

Winning Streak

Travis continued to win motocross races in 2000. He won five American Motorcyclist Association (AMA) Outdoor National events and became the AMA Outdoor National champion. Travis' success on the track earned him the AMA Rookie of the Year title. This award goes to the most successful newcomer to the sport.

Learn about:
- Winning races
- Doing tricks
- Paying the price

In 2000, Travis left other riders in the dust.

Travis helped the U.S. team win the Motocross des Nations in 2000.

In 2000, Travis competed in the Motocross des Nations in France. Travis and teammates Ricky Carmichael and Ryan Hughes raced against teams of riders from other countries. At age 17, Travis was the youngest member ever selected for the U.S. team. He didn't let his age hold him back. He helped the U.S. team win the race.

Gold Medal Streak

Travis has earned several gold medals in freestyle. In 1999, Travis won his first freestyle gold medal in the Summer X Games. He won the X Games gold again in 2000 and 2001, and Gravity Games gold medals in 1999 and 2001.

In the 2002 Gravity Games, Travis again won the gold medal. The crowd was awed by his backflips. However, the contest did not end well for him. He seriously injured his knee. He spent months recovering.

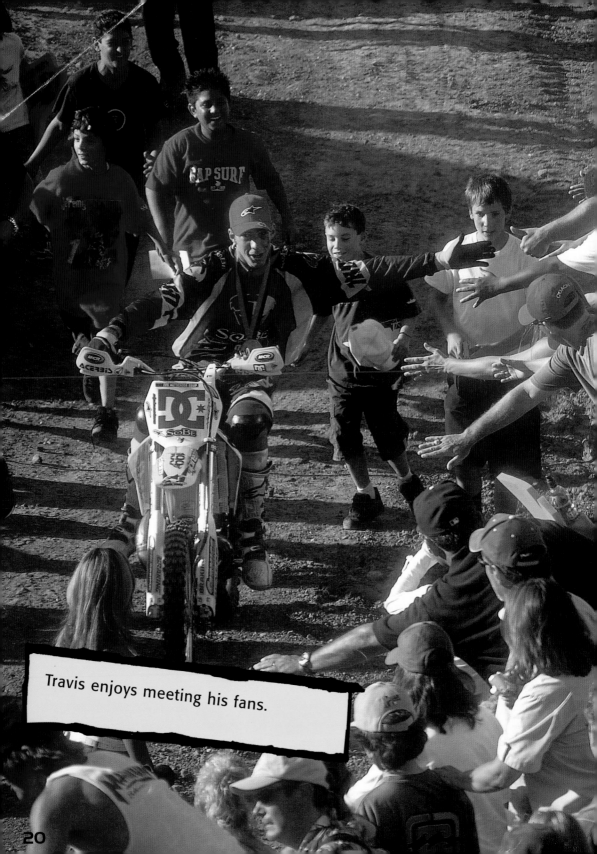

Travis enjoys meeting his fans.

Career
Statistics

Freestyle

Year	Competition	Event	Finish
1999	X Games	Freestyle	1st
2000	X Games	Freestyle	1st
2001	Gravity Games	Freestyle	1st
2001	X Games	Freestyle	1st
2002	Gravity Games	Freestyle	1st
2002	Gravity Games	FMX Challenge	1st
2003	X Games	Freestyle	1st
2003	Gravity Games	Freestyle	2nd
2003	Gravity Games	FMX Challenge	1st
2004	X Games	Freestyle	2nd

AMA Pro Racing

Year	Class	Wins	Points	Finish
2000	AMA Motocross 125cc	5	484	1st
2000	AMA East Supercross 125cc	2	164	3rd
2001	AMA Motocross 125cc	2	311	6th
2001	AMA East Supercross 125cc	5	154	1st

CHAPTER 4

Staying on Track

Travis raced hard, but he also crashed hard. By 2002, Travis had broken at least 30 bones. He also had 12 operations and 10 concussions.

Injuries prevented Travis from entering some races in 2003. He finished in 12th place in his best race of the year.

Learn about:

- Rally car racing
- Healing
- Having fun

Travis' daring style of riding often caused him to crash.

Travis' injuries continued. In June 2003, a car accident sent him to the hospital. He also crashed while trying to do a backflip at the 2003 Gravity Games. But he still won the silver medal.

Travis' injuries continued into the 2003 season.

A Break from Motocross

Some people thought Travis' injuries would force him to stop competing. Travis had other ideas. He looked into other sports, such as rally car racing. In this sport, Travis and a partner competed against other teams of drivers. They tried to be the first to finish an outdoor course. Travis' car got stuck in the snow a few times. That didn't stop him from enjoying the race. He finished in 19th place and was eager to improve.

Travis also competed in other sports. He finished 17th out of 500 riders in a motorcycle scramble on a hilly course in Austria. He raced in kart events, in a Porsche Cup car, and across the desert in a truck.

Travis Today

Travis is not one to let injuries get in his way. After his 2003 car accident, he went on to win a gold medal in freestyle at the 2003 X Games. In 2004, he won the silver.

Travis still likes to try new freestyle tricks and plans to keep competing. He wants to return to full-time motocross racing when his body heals. Most of all, he wants to keep having fun.

Travis enjoys having fun on his
motorcycle most of all.

Career Highlights

1999 – Travis wins the gold medal in freestyle motocross at the Summer X Games and the Gravity Games.

2000 – Travis wins the gold medal in freestyle motocross at the Summer X Games. He is also the AMA 125cc Outdoor Nationals champion and AMA Rookie of the Year. He is a member of the U.S. team that wins the Motocross des Nations.

2001 – Travis wins the AMA 125cc Eastern Region Supercross Series championship. He wins his third straight gold medal in freestyle motocross at the Summer X Games. He also wins the gold medal in freestyle at the Gravity Games.

2002 – Travis wins another gold medal in freestyle motocross at the Gravity Games.

2003 – Travis wins the silver medal in freestyle motocross at the Gravity Games. He wins gold at the Summer X Games.

2004 – Travis wins the silver medal in freestyle at the Summer X Games.

Glossary

amateur (AM-uh-chur)—an athlete who does not earn a living from competing in a sport

freestyle (FREE-stile)—a motorcycle contest involving stunts or tricks

motocross (MOH-toh-kross)—a sport in which people race motorcycles on dirt tracks

rookie (RUK-ee)—an athlete who is in his or her first season as a pro

scramble (SKRAM-buhl)—an off-road motorcycle race

supercross (SOO-puhr-kross)—motorcycle races held in a stadium

Read More

Blomquist, Christopher. *Motocross in the X Games.* A Kid's Guide to the X Games. New York: PowerKids Press, 2003.

Mahaney, Ian F. *Travis Pastrana: Motocross Champion.* Extreme Sports Biographies. New York: Rosen, 2005.

Sievert, Terri. *Dirt Bike History.* Dirt Bikes. Mankato, Minn.: Capstone Press, 2004.

Internet Sites

FactHound offers a safe, fun way to find Internet sites related to this book. All of the sites on FactHound have been researched by our staff.

Here's how:

1. Visit *www.facthound.com*
2. Type in this special code **0736843671** for age-appropriate sites. Or enter a search word related to this book for a more general search.
3. Click on the **Fetch It** button.

FactHound will fetch the best sites for you!

Index